THE VATICAN

ISBN 978-88-8271-222-8

© 2012 Edizioni Musei Vaticani
Città del Vaticano
www.museivaticani.va

Editorial direction: Direzione dei Musei

Copyediting: Ufficio Pubblicazioni Musei Vaticani

Photo credits:
Servizio Fotografico Musei Vaticani
Archivio Sillabe
Fabbrica di San Pietro in Vaticano (photos reproduced by kind permission, pp. 16, 18–29)
PubbliAerFoto (p. 6)

A publication by

s i l l a b e s.r.l.
scali d'Azeglio 22 - 57123 Livorno - Italia
www.sillabe.it - info@sillabe.it

Giunti Editore S.p.A.
via Bolognese 165 - 50139 Firenze - Italia
via Dante 4 - 20121 Milano - Italia
www.giunti.it

Management: Maddalena Paola Winspeare, Claudio Pescio
Texts: Nicola Bianchini
Design: Susanna Coseschi
Copy editing: Giulia Bastianelli

Translation: Catherine Burnett

Printed by Tipografia Vaticana

Reprint	Year
0 1 2 3 4 5 6 7 8 9	2012 2013 2014 2015 2016 2017 2018 2019 2020 2021

Nicola Bianchini

THE VATICAN

EDIZIONI MUSEI VATICANI

THE VATICAN

The Vatican City

The Vatican City State covers an area of just forty-four hectares, and with a total population of around eight hundred residents it is the smallest sovereign state in the world. Its borders are marked out by St. Peter's Square and the Leonine Walls (built by Pope Leo IV in the nineteenth century and then extended on several occasions). The boundaries lie entirely within the urban fabric of Rome and encircle St. Peter's Basilica, Palazzo Apostolico, Palazzo del Governatorato, the Vatican Museums and the Vatican Gardens as well as a number of other smaller buildings. Some areas beyond the borders also belong to the Vatican and are not part of the Italian State such as the Basilica of San Giovanni in Laterano, the Basilica of Santa Maria Maggiore and the papal residence of Castel Gandolfo.

The Vatican's institutional structure is that of an absolute monarchy as the Pope maintains legislative, executive and judicial power. The executive and administrative body of the State is called the Governorate (Governatorato). The Governor is a cardinal nominated by the Pope, who also represents the Pontiff in public functions.

The State was officially formed on 11 February 1929 under the Lateran Pacts between the Kingdom of Italy and the Holy See. The treaty recognised the respective independence and sovereignty of the two states and elevated the Papal State to a position guaranteed by the provisions of International Law. The document was signed by Benito Mussolini for the Italian State and Cardinal Pietro Gasperi for the Holy See and it provided a solution to the so-called Roman Question, a problem which had arisen after 20 September 1870 when the rifle regiment of the Italian Army (Bersaglieri) stormed Rome by force through the famous breach of Porta Pia. The troops occupied the city and confined the papal court to the Leonine City (within the Leonine Walls), though they spared the area from attack. In spite of attempts by the Italian State to restore and settle relations between the two institutions with the Law of Guarantees, the Pope still believed himself to be a prisoner and refused to sign any agreement with the King. The Lateran Pacts were amended in 1984 in the articles of the New Concordat signed by Cardinal Agostino Casaroli for Pope John Paul II and the President of the Council of Ministers, Bettino Craxi. The Vatican mint strikes its own currency, the euro, and issues postal stamps. Information sources include the daily newspaper "L'Osservatore Romano" and the radio station, Radio Vaticana. There is a police force for internal security and the historical corps of the Swiss Guards for the personal security of the Pope.

The Vatican also has a heliport and a short railway line linked to the Italian railway station of Roma San Pietro which was inaugurated in 1934.

Via Cornelia

- Circus of Nero
- Pagan Tomb
- Constantinian Basilica
- Current Basilica

A few steps back through history

The ancient name of the Vatican can be traced back to the Roman era and denoted a suburban marshy area which had long been surrounded by deep-rooted myths and legends.

During the Imperial era, when the marsh had been reclaimed, gardens were cultivated for the nobility and Emperor Caligula had a circus built to train charioteers which was later enlarged by Nero. Graveyards also sprang up along the main roads, one of which, along Via Cornelia, was discovered under the current St. Peter's Basilica and holds what is presumed to be the tomb of St. Peter. The presence of the apostle Peter had an irresistible appeal and his tomb became a place of pilgrimage leading to the rapid expansion of the burial ground. The entire area, however, was covered over in 324 AD when Emperor Constantine decided to level out the natural incline of the ground to construct a basilica dedicated to St. Peter; Constantine positioned the altar of the new basilica exactly over St. Peter's tomb.

Centuries later, to preserve the sanctity of the area, Pope Leo IV (847–855) built a fortified perimeter – the Leonine Walls – and under Eugene III (1145–1153) and Innocent III (1198–1216) construction work began within the enclosed area. At this point the Holy See was actually at the Basilica of San Giovanni in Laterano. It was only after the Avignon Papacy (1309–1377) that the Popes decided to reside permanently in the Vatican.

During the fifteenth century substantial extension projects were carried out on the whole complex. Sixtus IV (1471–1484) built the Great Chapel (Cappella Magna), better known as the Sistine Chapel, which was destined to become a universal temple of art. Innocent VIII (1484–1492) built Palazzetto del Belvedere and at the beginning of the following century, in 1506, Julius II (1503–1513) began construction work on the new St. Peter's Basilica on the site of the one-thousand-year-old Constantinian basilica which had become unstable.

As each century passed the magnificent complex of the Vatican Palaces grew in size and splendour along with the lovely gardens whose green and flowering lawns still cover the hill behind the basilica today. The most recently added architectural masterpieces include the Hall of Paul VI near St. Peter's Basilica, better known as the Nervi Hall after the architect who designed and built it between 1966 and 1971. This magnificent auditorium can hold up to twelve thousand people and contains Pericle Fazzini's monumental bronze sculpture of the *Resurrection of Christ* (1977).

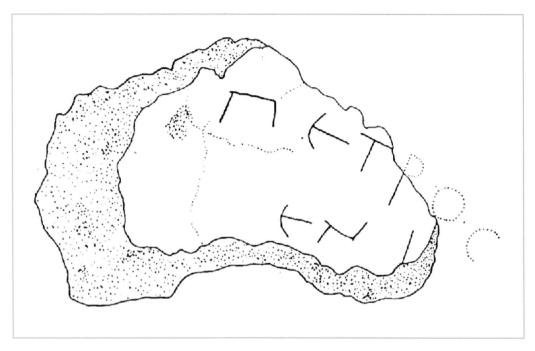

Graphic representation of a fragment of plaster from the Red Wall with the graffito inscription "Petros eni" (Peter is here)

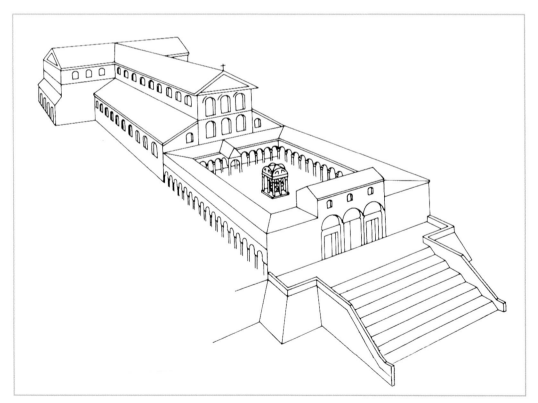

Representation of the Constantinian St. Peter's Basilica; the Pinecone Fountain is in the centre of the quadrangle

ST. PETER'S BASILICA

Constantinian Basilica

This large basilica, the centre and heart of Christianity, once stood above the tomb of the apostle Peter, who was martyred at Caligula's circus nearby during Nero's persecution of Christians in 64 AD. After decreeing freedom of worship in 313, Emperor Constantine ordered the construction of the first official sacred building in 324. It had a basilica-plan structure with five naves, an apse and a transept, and its floor area extended from the current presbytery almost to the façade built by Maderno. The high altar was positioned exactly above what was believed to be the apostle's tomb (as it is today in the current basilica).

The magnificent structure can hold an enormous number of worshippers and pilgrims. It was completed by a four-sided portico behind the façade known as the Portico of Paradise. A holy-water fountain stood in the centre of the portico, decorated with the famous bronze pinecone now in the Pinecone Courtyard in the Vatican Museums.

In order to prepare the site to build the Basilica, the slope of the Vatican hill had to be levelled off. It was for this reason that the roofs on the mausoleums along the avenues of the burial grounds had to be removed and the area completely covered over with earth. The interment actually conserved the superb stuccoes, paintings, sculptures and mosaics inside the mausoleums exceptionally well for almost two thousand years. The tombs have now been restored, but the microclimate around them has to be meticulously controlled to safeguard their state of conservation and visitor access is strictly limited. The age-old Constantinian basilica began to show significant signs of structural subsidence which became gradually worse over the course of the fifteenth century. To rectify the problem, Pope Nicholas V (1447–1455) asked Bernardo Rossellino to prepare a plan of action to save the building. The architect began construction on a new apse but the project, though already underway, was never completed.

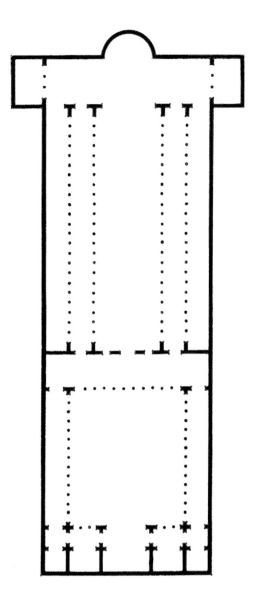

Bronze Pinecone in the Pinecone Courtyard, 1st–2nd century AD

Plan of the old St. Peter's Basilica

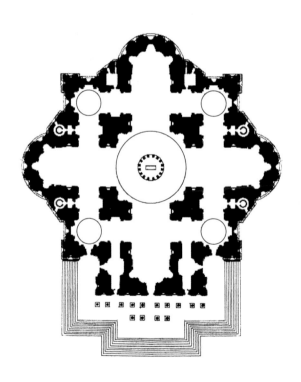

Plan of Donato Bramante's design (above) and Michel-angelo's design (below) for St. Peter's Basilica

New Basilica

At the beginning of his papacy, Pope Julius II (1503–1513) decided to entrust the construction of a new basilica to the ingenuity of Donato Bramante. The Pope climbed down into the foundation trenches and laid the first stone himself in 1506. In a substantial departure from traditional basilicas, the new building had a central-plan structure with an elegant geometric form based on a Greek cross drawn inside a square. Four mighty columns were conceived to support an enormous dome directly above St. Peter's tomb. Michelangelo had always been hard in his judgement of Bramante but even he praised the purity and linearity of his design. In actual fact, Bramante's ardour in pulling down the existing, ancient structure earned him the epithet of "Ruinante" ("the wrecker"). However that may be, when he died in 1514 the pillars of the dome were already in place. At this point, doubts began to emerge about how to continue the project. The Curia favoured a traditional basilica-plan structure so the new church would sit exactly on the same sacred spot as the Constantinian basilica. They also wanted to enlarge the surface area to increase the building's capacity. One of Bramante's successors, Raphael (also from Urbino), designed a new structure which incorporated the already-built pillars but lengthened the ground plan to the east and added three naves.

Raphael's idea, however, was not carried out either and over two unproductive decades passed until the arrival of Antonio da Sangallo the Younger. To Sangallo's mind, Bramante's design was not monumental enough so he began construction on ambulatories around the outer edges, divided the space inside with a series of inexplicable partition walls and devised a sort of longitudinal, barely defined main body as a nave. This project was carried out almost to the point of completion and it was harshly criticised by Michelangelo. He described all the additional walls as only creating 'lots of hiding places [...] that are exceedingly convenient for infinite wicked things: like secretly keeping bandits, making false money, getting nuns pregnant [...]'. As it was, when Michelangelo himself became the head architect of the St. Peter's worksite in 1547 he immediately ordered Sangallo's walls to be knocked down. He then simplified Bramante's design further, reducing the structure to its load-bearing components. The resulting design grew into an exceptionally elegant building, delicately shaped in stone and skilfully brought to life by chiaroscuro effects in the architectural ribbing.

13

Dome

Michelangelo designed the huge dome and when he died in 1564 the mighty drum was almost complete, supported by large twin columns. The honour of finishing construction (1588–1590) fell to Giacomo della Porta, who slightly modified the exterior when he raised the dome's original, perfectly semicircular line by seven metres, drawing closer to the more familiar and lauded shape of Brunelleschi's dome on the cathedral of Santa Maria del Fiore in Florence.

At one hundred and thirty-six metres high and forty-two metres wide, the impressive dome is estimated to weigh around fourteen thousand tonnes and it is constructed, like the dome in Florence, with a double vault. The inner vault is structural and the outer vault, which leans on the one below, has both a protective and aesthetic function. The hollow space in between helps the elasticity of the building and keeps the weight of the structure down. It also contains a staircase with five hundred and thirty-seven steps leading up to the lantern, which is seventeen metres high (as tall as a five storey building).

Carlo Maderno's extension and the façade

At the beginning of the seventeenth century the unresolved issue of the basilica's length arose once again and called into question Bramante and Michelangelo's central-plan designs. According to provisions made by the Council of Trent favouring a lengthened layout, Carlo Maderno was asked to give the church three naves and add three monumental bays, thus creating the largest building in Christendom (two hundred and eighteen metres long). The new façade, completed in 1614, was almost one hundred and fifteen metres wide. Columns and pilasters mark the tripartition of the church's interior and the Loggia of the Blessings lies in the centre (the balcony from which the election of the new pope is announced). A statue of Christ stands at the top above the attic, accompanied by John the Baptist and eleven of the apostles (St. Peter is missing). Two bell towers with clocks were designed to rise up on either side of the façade but in the end they were only built to the same height as the attic. There are six bells inside, the most famous of which is known as the *Big Bell* (*Campanone*) as it has a diameter of two metres and weighs almost nine tonnes.

The restoration for the Jubilee in 2000 uncovered the natural splendour of the travertine as well as the soft shade of colour chosen by Maderno. The original, almost mystical lines of Michelangelo's design were completely absorbed and effaced by the screen of the new façade and only Bernini's skill in the embrace of his colonnade partly recovered visibility by moving the viewpoint further away.

St. Peter's Square and the Colonnade

In 1657 work began on Gian Lorenzo Bernini's design for an adequately large area in front of the basilica and it led to great changes in the street layout of the ancient Borgo district.

Two straight and slightly converging wings were built from the edges of the basilica into the square, guiding and to some extent limiting the visual impact of Maderno's great façade. The two arms of the magnificent colonnade extend out and around the elliptic square – in the words of its creator – like an affectionate embrace. Bernini's design actually included a third wing across the wide opening to the east which left two small side entrances in line with the main roads of the area but because of a lack of available funds it was never built. The destruction of important historical buildings aligned with the façade (to make way for Via della Conciliazione) and the creation of Piazza Pio XII to replace the smaller Piazza Rusticucci shattered the equilibrium long sought by Bernini, spoiling the spectacular visual effect for whoever emerged from the little streets of the Borgo district into St. Peter's Square.

The ellipse is adorned with two large fountains and the Egyptian obelisk brought to Rome for Emperor Caligula (37–41 AD).

Portico

Before entering the basilica visitors pass through the large portico of the façade. There are two equestrian statues on each side: *Constantine* (on the right) by Gian Lorenzo Bernini (1670) and *Charlemagne* (on the left) by Agostino Cornacchini (1725). The basilica's five entrances are located on the main side. The central and most ancient entrance is faced by a mosaic called the *Navicella* (small ship), made from a design by Giotto for the Constantinian basilica and significantly reworked over the centuries. The door underneath is known as the Filarete Door after Antonio Averulino who was nicknamed Filarete (Greek for 'lover of excellence'). Averulino crafted the door for Pope Eugene IV between 1439 and 1445 for the old basilica. The six bronze panels hold depictions of Christ, the Virgin Mary and four episodes from the lives of St. Peter and St. Paul.

The *Door of the Sacraments* is the next entrance on the right followed by the famous *Holy Door* (only opened during jubilee years). The bronze *Holy Door* is by Vico Consorti (1950). On the opposite side, on the far left, there is an evocative masterpiece by Giacomo Manzù (1964) known as *Door of Death*. It is called the *Door of Death* because it is the portal through which the funeral cortege of deceased Popes passes. The bronze panels on the door depict themes linked to death: the deposition of Christ, the assumption of the Virgin, Eucharistic symbols and episodes of the death of Abel, Peter, John XXIII (the Pope who commissioned the door) and Gregory VII.

Gian Lorenzo Bernini, *Equestrian statue of Emperor Constantine*, 1670

on the left: Giacomo Manzù, *Door of Death*, 1964
on the right: Vico Consorti, *Holy Door*, 1950

Interior

The interior of the basilica is so vast that it astounds the senses of any visitor. It is over one hundred and eighty-seven metres long in total (the central nave is ninety metres long), twenty-six metres wide and around forty-five metres high. At the far end there is an immense open space under the dome, barely filled even by the magnificent baldachin Bernini constructed over the high altar. The lengths of the largest churches in Christendom are marked along the central nave towards the altar; all of which, in theory, are able to fit comfortably inside St. Peter's Basilica.

After admiring the size and harmonious beauty of this mighty building, visitors proceed along the right-hand nave.

The first chapel contains the famous *Pietà* sculpted by Michelangelo in 1499. This masterpiece reveals the height of the maestro's virtuosity and expresses, with unparalleled ability, the submissive pain of the Mother for her Child as he lies in her lap after he has been brought

down from the cross. Her pain is formed of silence, meditation and incomplete movements. The incomparable anatomic portrayal of Christ's body is undoubtedly down to the careful and secret studies the young artist carried out on cadavers in Florence. He dwells on the perfect aesthetic and functional form of the muscles, tendons and veins. Christ's lifeless body, laying in abandon, almost seems to melt into his mother's lap, close to her once again as if he were fading away in the soft and copious folds of her cloak. Mary's face was criticised at the time because it was thought to be implausibly young, but it only serves to express the incorruptible purity of the unblemished Virgin. Michelangelo sculpted this masterpiece when he was still a young and unknown artist and interestingly, he signed the work (on Mary's shoulder strap) some time after its completion to

Michelangelo Buonarroti, *Pietà*, 1499

silence the rumours that it had been done by Cristoforo Solari known as "il Gobbo".

Moving along the nave, the Chapel of St. Sebastian is decorated by Pietro da Cortona. It is followed by Bernini's monument to *Matilde di Canossa* and Maderno's large Chapel of the Holy Sacrament, conceived to connect the nave to the structure designed by Michelangelo. The chapel contains a gilded bronze tabernacle by Bernini (1674) and an altarpiece with the *Trinity* by Pietro da Cortona.

There is a must-see ancient bronze statue of *St. Peter Benedictory* near the pillar of the dome which historians attribute to Arnolfo di Cambio.

The large ambulatory around the open space under the dome marks the edge of the original ground plan of the basilica. The ambulatory holds a number of important monuments and altars. The altar of St. Jerome stands near the first pillar along the same line as the right-hand nave, and contains the mortal remains of Pope John XXIII; Antonio Canova's *Monument to Clement XIII* stands behind the right transept. On the other side there is a mosaic copy of Raphael's magnificent *Transfiguration* in the Clementine

Arnolfo di Cambio (attr.), *St. Peter Benedictory*, c. 1300

Antonio Canova, *Monument to Clement XIII*, 1758–1769

Chapel along with the remains of Gregory the Great and Pius VII. Bernini's last masterpiece, the *Monument to Pope Alexander VII*, stands behind the left transept. The artist sculpted this complex monument using different materials and colours between 1672 and 1678, two years before he died. The Pope at prayer is at the top, surrounded by the allegorical figures of *Charity* and *Truth* on the left and *Justice* and *Prudence* on the right. In the centre, from under a heavy drape in red marble, the lugubrious figure of a skeleton emerges with a clepsydra in his hand signifying the unstoppable passing of time on earth.

Gian Lorenzo Bernini, *Monument to Pope Alexander VII*, 1672–1678, whole and detail with *Charity* and *Prudence* in the foreground

24

Stop for a minute under the large dome in front of the bronze baldachin. Gian Lorenzo Bernini built the baldachin between 1624 and 1633 for Pope Urban VIII (Maffeo Barberini). It reaches a staggering height of almost thirty metres; the four spiral columns alone are eleven metres high. In order to cast the baldachin the ancient bronze statues on the façade and the bronze on the Pantheon's pronaos were removed and melted down. This gave rise to the famous lampoon 'Quod non fecerunt barbari, fecerunt Barberini" ("that which the barbarians did not do, the Barberini family did!') alluding to Pope Urban and the pillaged bronze.

The baldachin and the altar stand exactly over the presumed tomb of St. Peter, just as they had done in the previous basilica. The tomb is partially visible down the double ramp in front of the presbytery.

Bernini also crafted the reliquary of *St. Peter's Chair* in the apse.

Gian Lorenzo Bernini, *Bronze Baldachin*, 1624–1633

The reliquary surrounds what was presumed to be Peter's chair although in actual fact it is a throne from 875 given to John VIII. The reliquary is surmounted by sparkling rays, putti and golden clouds, inspired by the wonderful glazing on the window. The glazing effect is achieved with panels of thin alabaster and the dove of the Holy Spirit shines in the centre.

The inner sections of the four columns around the baldachin hold colossal statues of *St. Longinus* (Bernini, 1638), *St. Helena*, *St. Veronica* and *St. Andrew*.

Gian Lorenzo Bernini, *St. Peter's Chair*, 1656–1665

Gian Lorenzo Bernini, *St. Longinus*, 1638

The magnificent dome is split into sixteen segments and crystalline light floods like a waterfall through sixteen large windows. The mosaic decorations were done by Cavalier d'Arpino and Giovanni de Vecchi. They depict Christ, the apostles, and busts of popes and saints. The words along the face of the impost read: '*Tu es Petrus, et super hanc petram aedificabo Ecclesiam meam et tibi dabo claves regni Caelorum*' ('You are Peter, and upon this rock I will build my Church and I will give you the keys to the kingdom of heaven').

Moving back along the left-hand nave, the Chapel of the Choir is directly opposite and symmetrical to the Chapel of the Holy Sacrament. Both chapels have monumental gates crafted by Francesco Borromini.
The *Monument to Pius X* and the tomb of *Innocent VIII* by Antonio del Pollaiolo are followed by the Presentation Chapel and the *Monument to the Stuarts* by Antonio Canova. The visit comes to an end at the Baptistery behind the façade. The Baptistery was designed by Carlo Fontana and decorated with mosaics by Baciccio and Francesco Trevisani.

Vatican Grottoes

The crypt of the Vatican Grottoes lies under the central nave of the present basilica, just above the level of the ancient Constantinian basilica. Side chambers branch out from the main hall of this sacred site; the chambers contain the last resting places of a great number of popes, saints and sovereigns from the tenth century onwards, often in notable, artistic tombs. Noteworthy pieces include the *Monument to Boniface VIII* by Arnolfo di Cambio with the reclining figure of the pontiff; the tomb of *Sixtus IV* by Antonio del Pollaiolo; and the tombs of *Emperor Otto II* (died 983) and *Queen Christina of Sweden* (1626–1689).

The *Memoria Constantiniana* is a monument above Peter's tomb built to protect the saint's mortal remains. It stands in the apsidal area at the heart of the Grottoes. One of the chapels in the apse contains the *Madonna of the "Bocciata"* by Pietro Cavallini.

The name *"Bocciata"* (*Strike*) derives from an old legend about a drunken soldier who threw a bowl at the holy image after he had lost a game of bowls and caused the Virgin's face to swell.

Arnolfo di Cambio,
*Monument to
Boniface VIII*,
c. 1296–1300

Chapel of the Bocciata. On the altar, Pietro Cavallini,
Madonna of the Bocciata

St. Peter's Chapel with the *Memoria Constantiniana*

Pre-Constantinian Necropolis

This first-century AD necropolis lies below the level of the Grottoes and the old basilica in line with the central nave. It was discovered and explored between 1940 and 1957. It mostly contains mausoleum-style tombs, often with inner terraces and small enclosed courtyards, richly decorated with frescoes and stuccoes.

The visit comes to an end exactly under the dome at the *Campus Petri* ("Field P"). This area contains the Shrine against the Red Wall which is believed to be St. Peter's burial place. A lot of evidence points to this conclusion but absolute proof has never been found, partly due to the devotional site being violated during the first few centuries after its discovery.

The tombs are in an excellent state of conservation because they were sealed underground when the area was buried during the fourth century (to level off the slope of the Vatican Hill to build the Constantinian basilica). After these monuments were restored, a rigorous microclimate control system had to be installed to maintain a favourable environment for the extremely delicate decorations. Access to the necropolis is subject to a series of special regulations. A limited number of people can visit the site each day and booking is essential.

THE APOSTOLIC PALACE

Papal Palace

The Papal Palace (Palazzo Pontificio) is the name of the group of buildings which stand between St. Peter's Square and the northern perimeter wall of Paul III and Urban VIII (which now holds the entrance to the Vatican Museums).

Pope Nicholas III (1277–1280) oversaw the beginnings of the original complex. It was a turreted, quadrilateral structure around the Parrot Courtyard (Cortile del Pappagallo) which grew constantly over the following centuries and employed the most talented architects and artists from each era.

The Sistine Chapel, the Borgia Tower, the large Belvedere Courtyard designed by Bramante during Julius II's papacy, the new, elegant façade for the austere Palace of Nicholas III and the renowned Logge, completed and decorated by Raphael, were all part of this original quadrilateral structure.

Major construction projects ensued, in particular under Sixtus V who entrusted the construction of a new building to the east of the Courtyard of St. Damasus (the current Pope's residence) to Domenico Fontana.

Other monumental developments included the Royal Staircase (Scala Regia), superbly constructed by Gian Lorenzo Bernini to link the Royal Hall (Sala Regia) to the Atrium of St. Peter's Basilica. The ingenious architect skilfully adjusted the perspectival proportions of the staircase to create the impression of great depth and monumentality, far removed from its actual dimensions in view of the limited space available.

on page 30: View of the Sala Regia

Pauline Chapel

The Pauline Chapel is only a few metres away from the renowned Sistine Chapel, though unfortunately it is not part of the museum visit. Pope Paul III had the chapel built for his private use by Antonio da Sangallo the Younger and it owes its fame to the two frescoes on the walls by Michelangelo.

The frescoes were done between 1542 and 1550, a long period of time considering the relative size of the works. The artist, who was then in his seventies, had had several problems with his health which prevented him from working regularly on the two compositions. Furthermore, a fire broke out in the church in 1545 which hindered progress.

Michelangelo,
Conversion of Saul

Michelangelo,
*Crucifixion of
St. Peter*

The two masterpieces portray the *Conversion of Saul* and the *Crucifixion of St. Peter*. Though severely damaged over time, a recent restoration of the works has allowed us to rediscover and fully appreciate their abounding expressiveness and tormented spirituality. While Michelangelo was working on these frescoes he wrote poetry which dwelt heavily on death, an event he thought imminent. He also wrote about his crippling doubts as he approached the day of judgement before Christ, the same moment he had so passionately depicted a few years previously just two doors down from the Pauline Chapel. The artist's near obsession with these thoughts enhances our understanding of the importance he placed on depicting subjects and themes such as the conversion and death for faith.

MVSEI VATICANI

THE VATICAN MUSEUMS

Pinacoteca

Pope Benedict XIV opened the Capitoline Picture Gallery to the public on Capitoline Hill in 1748, although many long and unsettled years passed before the Vatican Pinacoteca was definitively established in the monumental building constructed by Luca Beltrami in 1932.

A few years later, in the Vatican, Clement XIV (1769–1774) and then Pius VI (1775–1799), began and developed a programme to reorganise the collections of classical sculptures and founded the Pius Clementine Museum. Consequently, the paintings in the Capitoline Picture Gallery were returned to the Vatican and formed the nucleus of the modern Pinacoteca. During Napoleon's occupation of Rome a great number of paintings were sent to France. After the fall of Napoleon and the Congress of Vienna, Antonio Canova travelled to Paris to recover the stolen items; there were five hundred and six paintings missing and less than half of them were returned to Rome.

The subsequent inadequacy of the exhibition areas in addition to overcrowding and the continual growth of the collections led to repeated relocations. A new Pinacoteca with two hundred and seventy-seven paintings from the Lateran and Vatican picture galleries and the ancient Vatican library was inaugurated in 1909 by Pope Pius X. The works were put on display following rational, chronological criteria which, for the time, was seen as very avant-garde.

There are now four hundred and sixty-three works on display in sixteen rooms in Beltrami's building. They form one of the largest collections in the world of Italian and European paintings from the twelfth century onwards.

Room I contains works by Italian painters from the twelfth and thirteenth centuries (known as the "primitives"). The paintings are mainly on wood with gold backgrounds.

Nicolaus and Johannes, *Last Judgement*
tempera on wood
late 12th century

This is the oldest work in the Pinacoteca and its iconography is fascinating. It has an unusual circular shape and shows Christ the Judge with episodes of the day of judgement below in ordered rows. The lower section shows the vision of New Jerusalem with the Virgin Mary, the souls of the just and a depiction of the damned in hell.

Room II is dedicated to Gothic painting and contains masterpieces of fourteenth-century Sienese painting. There are works by Simone Martini and Pietro Lorenzetti as well as Gentile da Fabriano and, above all, Giotto.

Giotto and assistants, *Stefaneschi Triptych*
tempera and gold on wood
c. 1320

This triptych is painted on both sides; the front shows St. Peter enthroned with St. James, St. Paul, St. Andrew and St. John the Evangelist and the back depicts Christ enthroned between scenes of the crucifixion of St. Peter and the decapitation of St. Paul. The artist's advanced understanding of perspective can be seen here in his depiction of the vanishing points of the steps up to the thrones and the solid physicality of the figures. Giotto's work formed a fundamental foundation for Renaissance painting.

Florentine art from the fourteenth and fifteenth centuries covers the walls of Room III with works by prominent Italian artists such as Fra Angelico, Benozzo Gozzoli and Filippo Lippi. The traditional gold background of the preceding era was used less and less until it disappeared all together in favour of naturalistic settings where the main figures come to life in believable poses and engage with their surroundings.

Fra Angelico, *Stories of St. Nicholas of Bari:*
Birth of St. Nicholas; Vocation; Gift to Three Poor Girls
St. Nicholas meets the Imperial Legate; St. Nicholas saves a Load of Grain for the City of Myra;
The Miraculous Saving of a Ship from Sinking
predella sections
tempera on wood
c. 1437

Filippo Lippi, *Coronation of the Virgin*
tempera on wood
c. 1444

Works by Melozzo da Forlì (1438–1494) are on display in Room IV. The exhibits are mainly fragments from the large fresco of the ascension of Christ painted for the apse of the Church of the Santi Apostoli in Rome. There is also a celebratory fresco of Pope Sixtus IV naming Platina as the first prefect of the Vatican Library. The fragments are characterised by extraordinary foreshortening and the depth in the fresco with Sixtus IV and Platina is perfectly rendered in perspective.

44

Melozzo da Forlì
Angel Musician and *Apostle*
detached fresco
c. 1480

TEMPLA DOMVM EXPOSITIS·VICOS FORA MOENIA PONTES·
VIRGINEAM TRIVII QVOD REPARARIS AQVAM·
PRISCA LICET NAVTIS STATVAS DARE COMMODA PORTVS·
ET VATICANVM CINGERE SIXTE IVGVM·
PLVS TAMEN VRBS DEBET·NAM QVAE SQVALORE LATEBAT·
CERNITVR IN CELEBRI BIBLIOTHECA LOCO·

Melozzo da Forlì, *Sixtus IV and Platina*
detached fresco transferred to canvas
c. 1477

A particularly significant work amongst the fifteenth-century Italian paintings in Room V is the elaborate predella by Ercole de' Roberti; the episodes are set in complex scenes full of classical architecture and ruins reflecting the penchant for the ancient which was popular at the time. They are portrayed in an imaginary setting where the landscape and the buildings seem to fuse together into a single, surreal panorama.

Ercole de' Roberti, *Miracles of St. Vincent Ferrer*:
Healing of the lame woman, Raising of a rich Jewish woman from the dead, Saving of a child from a house on fire, Raising from the dead of a child killed by his pregnant, lunatic mother, Healing of an injured person
predella of the *Griffoni Polyptych*
tempera on wood
1473

Room VI contains monumental fifteenth-century polyptychs with elaborate carpentry, typical tokens of religious devotion at the time. Carlo Crivelli's signed and dated (1482) *Madonna and Child* is particularly incisive. Crivelli was a prolific Venetian painter although very little is actually known about his life.

Carlo Crivelli, *Madonna and Child*
tempera on wood
1482

Paintings of the Umbrian school are on display in Room VII including the *Madonna and Child with St. Herculanus, St. Constant, St. Lawrence and St. Louis of Toulouse*. The vaulted arch and the monumental throne are both perfectly rendered in perspective. The throne stands out in the centre with the artist's name inscribed along the base.

Pietro Perugino, *Madonna and Child with St. Herculanus, St. Constant, St. Lawrence and St. Louis of Toulouse*
tempera on wood
1496

Works by the great Raffaello Sanzio (Raphael) are in display in Room VIII. Besides the magnificent altarpieces, the *Scuola Vecchia* (Old School) tapestries are particularly noteworthy. They were woven from cartoons by Raphael with episodes from the lives of St. Peter and St. Paul. Leo X commissioned the tapestries from the artist in 1515 for the side walls of the Sistine Chapel.

Raphael, *Coronation of the Virgin (Oddi Altarpiece)*
tempera on wood transferred to canvas
1502–1504

The iconography in this early work by Raphael is set on two levels: the lower section depicts the apostles around the Virgin Mary's empty grave and the upper section shows Christ crowning Mary on a cloud in the sky, surrounded by angel musicians and cherubs.

Raphael, *Madonna of Foligno*
tempera on wood transferred to canvas
1511–1512

The buyer of this painting, Sigismondo de' Conti, is depicted kneeling in a red cloak with St. John the Baptist, St. Francis and St. James. Sigismondo was meant to tell Raphael why he had commissioned the work but he died before he had the chance to explain. Consequently, the cartouche held up by the angel in the centre remained empty. Historians tend to describe the work as a votive offering, perhaps in reference to a lucky escape from the meteorite which is depicted falling on one of the houses in the little town in the background.

Flemish manufacture by Pieter van Aelst from a cartoon by Raphael, *Miraculous Draft of Fish*
tapestry
1515–1519

Raphael, *Transfiguration*
tempera on wood
1517–1520

This masterpiece may have been conceived as a result of Raphael's rivalry with Sebastiano del Piombo.
Its iconography is both unusual and complex. The upper section shows the transfiguration of Christ in the
presence of Moses and Elijah. The apostles Peter, James and John lay on the ground bewildered by the
extraordinary event. The lower section depicts the healing of a wild-eyed possessed boy with bold use of
narrative techniques.

Room IX is dominated by the painting on wood of *St. Jerome*, an unfinished masterpiece by Leonardo da Vinci. Other noteworthy exhibits include Giovanni Bellini's *Lamentation over the Dead Christ*, characterised by an intangible silence, immobility, composure and concentration which is typical of the Venetian maestro's style.

Giovanni Bellini, *Lamentation over the Dead Christ with St. Joseph of Arimathea, St. Nicodemus and Mary Magdalene*
oil on wood
c. 1471–1474

Leonardo da Vinci, *St. Jerome*
oil on wood
c. 1482

This painting, of unknown origin, is characterised by an aura of mystery enhanced by the rugged and mysterious desert landscape of strangely-shaped, sharp rocks and the evanescent figure of the hermit saint. The emaciated St. Jerome beats his chest with a stone in penitence. The lion at his feet, as tradition has it, became loyal to the saint after he managed to remove a painful thorn from its paw.
As the composition remains unfinished, the maestro's strong strokes of the preparatory drawing are clearly visible.

Room X contains skilful paintings of the Venetian school. Particularly noteworthy exhibits include Titian's large altarpiece of the *Madonna and Child with Saints ("Madonna of the Frari")* and Veronese's superb *Vision of St. Helena*.

Titian, *Madonna and Child with Saints ("Madonna of San Niccolò dei Frari al Lido")*
oil on wood transferred to canvas
1533–1535

Although the upper section of this painting is missing – probably a scene with the soaring dove of the Holy Spirit – it is still a magnificent composition. The Madonna and Child surrounded by angels sit above on a cloud, separated from the saints below. The superb figure of St. Catherine stands on the left followed by St. Nicholas, St. Peter, St. Anthony, St. Francis and St. Sebastian.

Paolo Caliari known as Veronese, *Vision of St. Helena*
oil on canvas
c. 1580

As tradition has it, Emperor Constantine's mother, St. Helena, had a vision which led to the discovery of the True Cross. Veronese portrays the story as a dream; the sleeping figure of St. Helena, her head resting on her hand, lets the artist focus on the composition's supple lines, the rich brocade of the dress and the detailed embroidery on the walls. In the dream, a little angel on the right appears with the cross.

Italian paintings from the second half of the sixteenth century are on display in Room XI. Must-see exhibits include the *Flight into Egypt* and the *Annunciation* by Federico Barocci. In the *Flight into Egypt* every trace of the dramatic force of the escape is softened by the warm intimacy of the family, safe on the edge of a valley and enjoying the fruit which providence has placed in their path.

Federico Barocci, *Flight into Egypt ("Madonna of the Cherries")*
oil on canvas
1570–1573

Jacopo Zucchi, *Miracle of the Snow*
oil on wood
c.1573-1575

Room XII is dedicated to the great Caravaggio. It also contains works by early seventeenth-century painters strongly influenced Caravaggio's work in the search for new realism and bolder use of perspective. Besides Caravaggio's masterpiece, the *Deposition*, other noteworthy exhibits include the *Crucifixion of St. Peter* and the *St. Matthew and the Angel* by Guido Reni, the *Communion of St. Jerome* by Domenichino, and the *St. Mary Magdalene Penitent* by Guercino.

Caravaggio, *Deposition*
oil on canvas
1600–1604

The iconography in this painting is revolutionary, dominated by the skilful use of sculptural light. It realistically portrays the moment between the deposition of Christ and the approaching closure of the tomb. The tragic and dramatic scene is illuminated by the great theological message of the resurrection: the bright white shroud casts an unfathomable light of hope which tears into the darkness of the background and defies death, just as the sharp edge of the tombstone calls to mind the evangelical verse: "The stone the builders rejected has become the cornerstone".

Domenichino, *Communion of St. Jerome*
oil on canvas
1614

Guercino, *St. Mary Magdalene Penitent*
oil on canvas
1622

Guido Reni, *St. Matthew and the Angel*
oil on canvas
1635–1640

The works on display in Room XIII can be dated to the seventeenth century. The paintings by Pietro da Cortona are particularly noteworthy including the renowned *Vision of St. Francis*, an only slightly smaller copy of the altarpiece for the Church of the Santissima Annunziata in Arezzo. The bloody realism of Orazio Gentileschi's *Judith and her Maidservant with the Head of Holofernes* makes the scene particularly effective.

Orazio Gentileschi, *Judith and her Maidservant with the Head of Holofernes*
oil on canvas
1611–1612

Pietro da Cortona, *Vision of St. Francis*
oil on canvas
c. 1641

Room XIV contains various paintings from different European schools which can be dated to between the seventeenth and eighteenth centuries and include some charming still-life scenes attributed to Pietro Navarra.

Pietro Navarra (?), *Still Life*
oil on canvas

Room XV contains various official portraits including the *Portrait of Pius VI* by Pompeo Batoni and the *Portrait of George IV of England* by Thomas Lawrence. Intense psychological depth pervades the impressive *Portrait of Clement IX* by Carlo Maratta. There is also a series of fascinating *Astronomical Observations* by Donato Creti.

Pompeo Batoni, *Portrait of Pius VI*
oil on canvas
1775

Carlo Maratta, *Portrait of Clement IX*
oil on canvas
1669

Donato Creti, *Astronomical Observations*
oil on canvas
1711

Room XVI is dedicated to the Bohemian painter Wenzel Peter. It is dominated by large paintings of wild animals and the enormously detailed, stunning depiction of *Adam and Eve in the Garden of Eden*.

Wenzel Peter, *Fight of a Lion with a Tiger*
oil on canvas

Wenzel Peter, *Adam and Eve in the Garden of Eden*
oil on canvas

Pinecone Courtyard

In 1506, as part of a vast restructuring programme, Pope Julius II entrusted plans for the hill between Innocent VIII's Palazzetto del Belvedere (used as a summer residence) and the Vatican Palaces to Donato Bramante. The architect designed two long parallel wings with several floors and terraces linked by large ramps to resolve the issue of the sloping ground. The large enclosed area in the centre, used for jousts and games, was split in two at the end of the sixteenth century under Sixtus V with a transversal wing designed by Carlo Fontana to hold the Vatican Library. Later, the area was further reduced on the northern side with the construction of another transversal building called the New Wing (Braccio Nuovo), built to hold a collection of classical sculptures. The three resulting courtyards are the Pinecone Courtyard, the Library Courtyard and the Belvedere Courtyard. The Pinecone Courtyard, the only one accessible to the public though the Museums, is named after the large bronze pinecone which sits on one side and was originally part of a huge Roman-era fountain. In the Middle Ages it was placed in the four-sided portico behind the Constantinian St. Peter's Basilica, and then moved here in 1608 when the new basilica was being enlarged.

Arnaldo Pomodoro
Sphere Within Sphere
bronze
1990

The sculpture *Sphere Within Sphere* (1990) by Arnaldo Pomodoro stands in the middle of the courtyard and, to the south, the Tower of the Winds rises up to one side of the New Wing where it joins the main building.

Chiaramonti Museum and Lapidary Gallery

The Chiaramonti Museum is set in an ancient gallery designed by Bramante and holds a copious collection of Roman-era sculptures, placed here under Pope VII Chiaramonti by Antonio Canova, the Inspector General of Fine Arts and Antiquities of the Papal States. The monumental corridor contains hundreds of sculptures, many of which are original masterpieces of ancient art such as *Ganymede and the Eagle* and the monumental head of *Athena*, thought to be a Roman copy of the *Athena Promachos* by Phidias.

The Chiaramonti Museum leads into the long Lapidary Gallery which holds one of the most important collections in the world – initiated under Pope Benedict XIV – of Latin and Greek epigraphy.

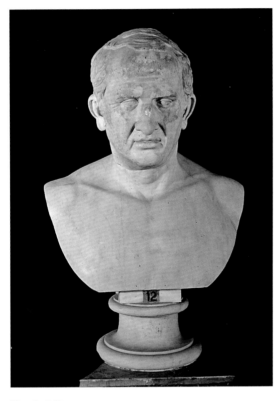

72 *Head of Cicero*
probable Trajan era copy of a famous figure from the
late Republican era thought to be Marcus Tullius Cicero
(106–43 BC)
Wall XI

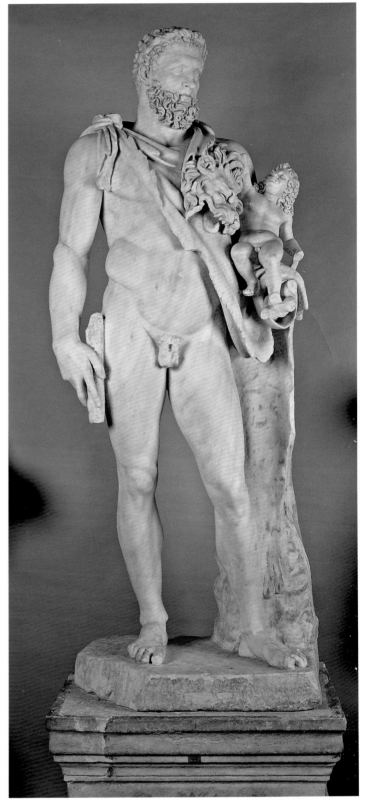

Statue of Heracles with young Telephus
Trajan era copy after a late Hellenistic original
Wall IX

New Wing

In 1806 Pope Pius VII ordered the construction of the so-called New Wing (Braccio Nuovo) as an extension to the Chiaramonti Museum. Raffaele Stern designed the new building and created a perfect setting for the museum's masterpieces of ancient Roman statuary.

Some of the most important works on display include the *Augustus of Prima Porta*, the renowned portrait of the first Roman Emperor with his magnificent *lorica* (decorated armour used by the Roman army) as he delivers an *Adlocutio* (the speech which generals gave to their troops to encourage them before battle); the *Nile*, the monumental personification of the great river portrayed as a reclining bearded man surrounded by sphinxes and crocodiles evoking the geographical position of the river, and children which allude to its fertility; and the Roman copy of the *Doryphorus* by Polycletus (*c.* 440 BC), a work which, since antiquity, has rightfully been regarded as absolute perfection in the portrayal of the human body.

74

Augustus of
Prima Porta
early 1st century AD

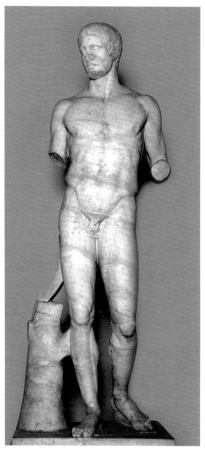

Silenus
mid-2nd century AD Roman copy after a Greek original by
Lysippos from *c.* 300 BC

Statue of Doryphorus
Roman copy after a Greek bronze
original by Polycletus from 440 BC

Statue of the Nile
1st century AD after
a Hellenistic original
from the Temple of
Isis and Serapis in
Rome

Pius-Clementine Museum

The oldest and most evocative part of the Vatican Museums lies in the Pius-Clementine Museum, in particular in the Octagonal Courtyard, the current location of the very first pieces of illustrious ancient art collected by Julius II such as the *Apollo* and the *Laocoon*.
The visitor route around this museum was modified at the end of the eighteenth century by Clement XIV and Pius VI. The sculptures were positioned in classical, evocative architectural settings and enchanting rooms which now hold world-renowned masterpieces such as the *Apoxyomenos*, the marble "zoo" in the Room of the Animals, the *Venus Felix*, the *Ariadne Sleeping*, and famous *Belvedere Torso* which fascinated Michelangelo.

Venus Felix
2nd-century AD Roman copy after
the *Aphrodite of Cnidus* by Praxiteles
(4th century BC)
Octagonal Courtyard

Apoxyomenos
1st-century AD Roman copy after
a 4th-century BC bronze original
Octagonal Courtyard, Apoxyomenos Cabinet

Laocoon
1st-century AD copy after a 2nd-century BC Greek original
Octagonal Courtyard, Laocoon Cabinet

Apollo Belvedere
2nd-century AD Roman copy
after a 4th-century BC original
Octagonal Courtyard, Apollo
Cabinet

Statue Gallery

Ariadne Sleeping
2nd-century AD
Roman copy after a
2nd-century BC original
Statue Gallery

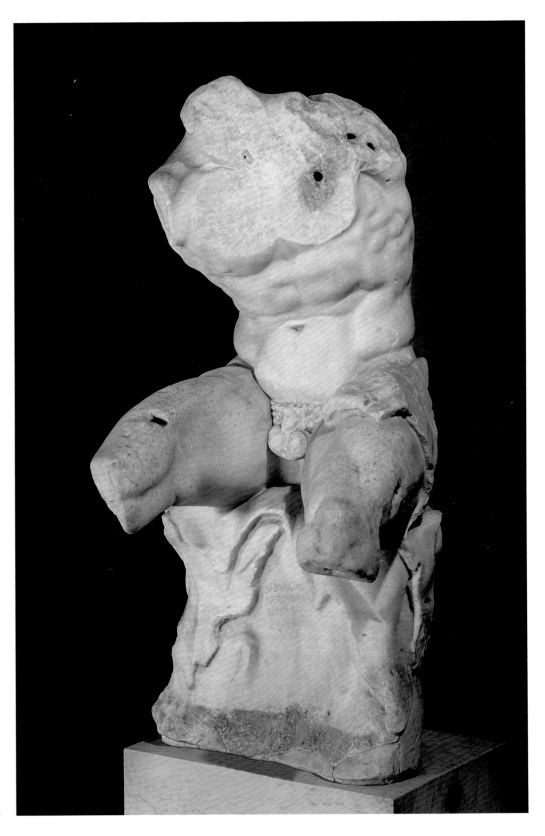

Belvedere Torso
1st century BC
Room of the Muses

Round Room

Greek Cross Room

Gregorian Egyptian Museum

This collection of Egyptian artefacts was arranged for display by the Barnabite father and Egyptologist Luigi Maria Ungarelli, who also planned the decorations in the rooms with explicit references to ancient Egyptian art such as columns with lotus flowers, eyes of Ra and open wings of the god Horus.

The collection includes pharaonic statues imported as early as Roman antiquity as well as later acquisitions and donations. The Museum was inaugurated in 1839 under Pope Gregory XVI.

Some of the most important works include the sculptural fragment of *Ramses II enthroned*, the sarcophagi, two mummies and the collection of canopic vases as well as the colossal statues of Egyptian gods and Queen Tuya (Seti I's wife and Ramses II's mother).

The last part of the museum is dedicated to Mesopotamian culture with letters in cuneiform script, seals and royals stamps as well as fragments of reliefs with battle scenes.

*Memorial Stele of Hatshepsut and
Thutmose III*
from Thebes
18th dynasty, *c.* 1460 BC
Room I

Statue of Queen Tuya
from Thebes
19th dynasty, 1291–1185 BC
Hemicycle

*Case and Lid of the
Sarcophagus of
Djet-Mut*
from Thebes
21st dynasty,
1000 BC
Room II

Gregorian Etruscan Museum

The collections of the Gregorian Etruscan Museum were first gathered together at the beginning of the nineteenth century after the influx of findings discovered during the prolific excavation projects carried out in Etruscan areas (then part of the Papal States). The findings were prepared for display in 1837 under Pope Gregory XVI.

The collection documents artistic and manufacturing production from the whole of Etruscan history from the first Villanovan period (tenth to ninth century BC) to the annexation of Etruria to the rule of Rome. It includes a remarkably interesting set of objects found intact in the Regolini Galassi tomb discovered at Cerveteri in 1836, and the *Mars of Todi*, the renowned bronze sculpture inspired by great Greek statuary.

The museum continues with an *antiquarium* containing a selection of Roman findings which were originally thought to be Etruscan. It then comes to a close with a rich display of painted ceramics. Noteworthy masterpieces on display here include an attic black-figure amphora signed by the famous painter Exekias depicting Achilles and Ajax playing dice.

86

Gold Fibula
mid-7th century BC
Room II

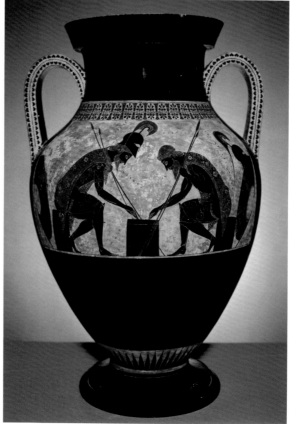

"Calabresi" Urn (House-Shaped Cinerary Urn with a Lid)
second half of the 7th century BC
Room II

Exekias, *Black-Figure Attic Amphora*
540–530 BC
Room XIX

88

Mars of Todi
bronze, late
5th century BC
Room III

Biga Room

This room lies above the Atrium of the Four Gates and was built by Giuseppe Camporesi in 1786 in a classical architectural style.

In the centre of the room, under the lacunar ceiling, there is a marble *Biga* (two-horse chariot) which dates back to the first century AD. Francesco Antonio Franzoni completed the chariot when it was put on display by adding the wheels, the shaft and one of the horses.

A number of classical sculptures also stand in this room, superb Roman copies of Greek originals. Noteworthy pieces include the *Dionysus "Sardanapalus"*, a Roman copy of a Greek original from the school of Praxiteles (late fourth century BC) and a Trajan-era marble copy of Myron's bronze *Discobolus* (*c.* 460 BC).

*Two-Horse Chariot
(Biga)*
1st century AD
Roman art

Gallery of Candelabras

Originally an open loggia, this gallery was closed off under Pope Pius VI by the architect Michelangelo Simonetti. It now holds many exquisitely-made classical Greek and Roman sculptures. It is named after the pairs of marble candelabras at the beginning of each bay in the gallery.

Gallery of Tapestries

Originally conceived as a picture gallery, this room has held a series of wall-hangings known as the *Scuola Nuova* (*New School)* tapestries since 1838. The name *Scuola Nuova* distinguishes the works from the *Scuola Vecchia* (*Old School)* tapestries from Leo X's time, designed by Raphael for the Sistine Chapel. The *Scuola Nuova* tapestries were also woven in Brussels, albeit later under Clement VII, based on cartoons by Raphael's pupils. They portray episodes from the *Life of Jesus* from the *Nativity* to the *Dinner at Emmaus*. A series of tapestries depicting the *Life of Urban VIII* is also on display in the gallery.

Death of Caesar
Flemish
Manufacture by
Pieter van Aelst,
Brussels, 1549

Gallery of Maps

This long gallery was commissioned by Pope Gregory XIII from the architect Ottaviano Mascherino, who carried out the building work between 1578 and 1580. Girolamo Muziano and Cesare Nebbia oversaw the completion of the ambitious decorative design for the gallery.

The walls hold forty geographical maps of Italy from north to south. They are set on the walls according to their position next to either the Tyrrhenian and Ligurian Seas or the Adriatic Sea and the Alpine arch. The frescoed maps were created from drawings by Ignazio Danti, one of the foremost cosmographers of the time. As well as the geopolitical portrayal of the regions, there are also illustrations of important historical events in the areas in which they took place. Using the same approach, the panels on the ceiling narrate prominent episodes from the history of the Church which are linked to the corresponding geographical regions below.

Evil Theodoric cast into the volcano through the gates of hell
ceiling of the Gallery of Maps

Ignazio Danti
Italia antiqua

Latium et Sabina (southern Lazio), detail with the city of Rome

Sobieski Room and
Room of the Immaculate Conception

The Sobieski Room is named after a large painting by Jan Matejko (1838–1893) of the King of Poland, John III Sobieski, who defeated the Turks at Vienna in 1683.

The Room of the Immaculate Conception in the Borgia Tower nearby was decorated by the painter Francesco Podesti for Pope Pius IX in 1858 to celebrate the promulgation of the dogma of the Immaculate Conception of Mary (proclaimed on 8 December 1854).

The large frescoes depict the *Promulgation of the Dogma of the Immaculate Conception*, the *Discussion of the Immaculate Conception*, the *Coronation of the Image of the Immaculate Conception* and *Stories and Allegorical Figures*. A precious display case by Christofle of Paris in the centre of the room holds the text of the Papal bull, translated into the main world languages.

Raphael's Rooms

Raphael's Rooms, or *Stanze* as they are known in Italian, are on the second floor of the Papal Palace in the apartment chosen by Julius II della Rovere and then Leo X as their residence. Pope Julius first asked Perugino and Luca Signorelli to fresco the area, but the final decoration of the rooms and the consequent partial destruction of the previous frescoes was carried out by Raphael and his studio between 1508 and 1524.

The first room to be frescoed was the Room of the Signature (1508–1511) which holds Raphael's most famous frescoes and takes its name from the highest tribunal of the Holy See, the "Signatura Gratiae et Iustitiae". The iconographical layout is based on the supreme concepts of Truth, Goodness, Justice and Beauty. Truth is exalted through Theology and Philosophy (supernatural truth in the *Disputation of the Holy Sacrament*, rational truth in the *School of Athens*); Goodness based on Justice is celebrated through the Law (in the *Theological and Cardinal Virtues* and in the institution of the fundamental codices of the *Corpus Juris Civilis* of

Raphael
School of Athens
whole and detail of
Plato and Aristotle
Room of the Signature

98

Justinian, the Decretals of Canonical Legislation); and finally, under the influence of Apollo playing the cithara embodying music and poetry, the wall with the *Parnassus* glorifies Beauty revealed through the writings of the great poets from Homer and Dante to Petrarch and Ariosto.

The Room of Heliodorus was used for the Pope's private audiences. The frescoes, therefore, hold connotations which are both religious and political and aim to illustrate the protection accorded by God to his Church. The *Expulsion of Heliodorus from the Temple* symbolically shows the safeguarding of the patrimony of St. Peter (one of Julius II's unwavering objectives); the *Mass at Bolsena* shows the defence of the faith; the *Liberation of St. Peter* reveals the protection accorded by Providence to the Pope; and the *Meeting between St. Leo I the Great and Attila* shows the safeguarding of the Holy See in Rome.

During Julius II's papacy the Room of the Fire was used as the seat of the highest tribunal of the Papal Curia. The original purpose of the room is reflected in the frescoes on the ceiling painted by Perugino. Under Leo X de' Medici the room became the Pope's private luncheon room and the Pontiff asked Raphael to decorate it. The frescoes illustrate the political aspirations of Leo X and exalt his papacy through stories from the life of two of his ancient predecessors of the same name: Leo III (the *Coronation of Charlemagne* and the *Justification of Leo III*) and Leo IV (the *Fire in the Borgo* and the *Battle of Ostia*).

Raphael
Disputation of the Holy Sacrament
Room of the Signature

Raphael
Parnassus
Room of the Signature

Raphael
Liberation of
St. Peter
whole and detail of
the Angel in prison
with Peter
Room of Heliodorus

on the following
pages:
Room of the Fire

Finally the Hall of Constantine, the largest room in the whole apartment, was frescoed by Rapha-el's pupils after his death (1520) partly based on designs by the maestro. It was intended for offi-cial receptions and ceremonies and takes its name from Constantine, the first Roman emperor to officially recognise the Christian religion by conceding freedom of worship. The iconographic de-sign follows the same criteria of the celebration of the Church present in all the rooms, portrayed here in the emphatic defeat of paganism and the triumph of the Christian religion (the *Apparition of the Cross*, the *Battle of Milvian Bridge*, the *Baptism of Constantine* and the *Donation of Rome*). The allegorical scene of the *Triumph of Christianity* frescoed by Tommaso Laureti on the ceiling of this room is even clearer in meaning; Christ's cross is raised up on a small altar above a broken statue of a pagan divinity, symbolising the death of pagan idols.

Raphael
*Expulsion of
Heliodorus from
the Temple*
Room of Heliodorus

Raphael
Fire in the Borgo,
whole and detail
of female figures
carrying water jugs
Room of the Fire

Chapel of Nicholas V

All that remains of the decorations in the Papal Palace from the time of Nicholas V is the magnificent Chapel of Nicholas V (*Cappella Niccolina*), built in a mediaeval tower and decorated by Fra Angelico in collaboration with Benozzo Gozzoli between 1447 and 1450. Situated in the most isolated wing of the papal apartment and intended for the private or semi-private use of the Pope, this chapel can be accessed through a small adjoining room which Julius II used as his bed chamber (*cubiculum*). The small chapel is frescoed on two levels with scenes from the lives of St. Lawrence and St. Stephen. The decorations also include figures of the *Doctors of the Church* and, on the ceiling, the *Four Evangelists*.

View of the entrance wall
and the east wall

Fra Angelico, Ceiling of the
Chapel of Nicholas V with the
Four Evangelists

Fra Angelico
Sermon of
St. Stephen

Fra Angelico
Capture and
Stoning of
St. Stephen, whole
and detail of the
capture of the saint

Raphael's Loggia

Raphael's Loggia is on the second floor of an elegant building overlooking the Courtyard of Damasus. It is adjoined by two of Raphael's Rooms, the Hall of Constantine and the Chiaroscuro Room. Donato Bramante designed and oversaw the initial construction of the Loggia but when the architect died in 1514 Raphael took over. He based the designs for the frescoes on episodes from the Old Testament and they came to be known collectively as "Raphael's Bible". At around the same time, Michelangelo was painting the ceiling of the Sistine Chapel. The spirited grotesques are by Giovanni da Udine and Perin del Vaga, inspired by the decorative work in Nero's Domus Aurea.

Borgia Apartment

Situated on the first floor of the Papal Palace below Raphael's Rooms, this apartment was used by Rodrigo de Borja y Doms, or rather Pope Alexander VI (1492–1503) as his private residence. The decorative work was entrusted to Pinturicchio and his studio. Between 1492 and 1494, the artist conceived and completed a series of scenes with extraordinarily complicated and exceptional iconography, inspired by the rich colours and classical-style compositions in the Domus Aurea. The rooms in the Borgia Apartment are traditionally known by names based on the thematic compositions on the walls: the Room of the Mysteries, the Room of the Saints, the Room of the Liberal Arts, the Room of the Creed and the Room of the Sibyls. The Borgia Apartment reflects the tastes of the Pope who commissioned the work including his interest in antiquarian culture, which Pinturicchio ingeniously interpreted and popularised. It is probable that Annio di Viterbo, a scholar and distinguished humanist in the service of the Pope, was responsible for the complicated iconographic code of the frescoes.

*Room of the
Mysteries*

Pinturicchio and his
school, *The Ceiling*
Room of the Creed

Collection of Contemporary Art

The Borgia Rooms now temporarily hold part of the Collection of Contemporary Art inaugurated by Pope Paul VI in 1973. The vast collection is set in fifty-five rooms of the Vatican Museums. It fills the apartments of Innocent III, Sixtus V and Alexander VI Borgia and almost reaches the threshold of the Sistine Chapel. The collection contains around seven hundred paintings, drawings and sculptures by almost two hundred and seventy artists including Vincent van Gogh, Auguste Rodin, Paul Gauguin, Wassily Kandinsky, Marc Chagall, Paul Klee, Giorgio de Chirico, Giorgio Morandi, Renato Guttuso, Pablo Picasso, Salvador Dalí and Giacomo Manzù; an anthology of nineteenth and twentieth-century works of art which is virtually unparalleled in Italy.

Maurice Denis,
Angels, 1901

Vincent van Gogh, *Pietà*, *c.* 1890

Sistine Chapel

This mediaeval chapel was enlarged between 1477 and 1481 for Sixtus IV della Rovere using the same proportions as the Temple of Jerusalem. Crenellated battlements were also added to the exterior of the new structure.

The decorative work inside forms one of the greatest and most complex sacred pictorial cycles in the world and is the result of intensely profound theological thinking. It must be interpreted as a whole even though different artists worked on the scenes at different times. The cycle narrates God's great investment in humanity and His message of salvation over the centuries from the Genesis and the pact with the Israelites to the new alliance and the coming and sacrifice of Christ. Michelangelo's magnificent, final scene of the *Last Judgement* prefigures Christ's last coming, when humanity will be judged before entering the afterlife.

The fifteenth-century decorations on the walls were frescoed by masters of the Renaissance between 1481 and 1483 and include trompe l'oeil drapes, the *Stories of Moses*, the *Stories of Christ* and above, the portraits of the *Popes*. The screen and the choir by Mino da Fiesole also date back to this period.

In 1508 Pope Julius II della Rovere asked Michelangelo to paint the ceiling with a new decorative cycle inspired by the stories in the Book of Genesis from creation and original sin to the great flood and the rebirth of humankind through Noah and his family. Michelangelo frescoed five *Sibyls* and seven *Prophets* in-between the spandrels; the *Ancestors of Christ* in the spandrels and lunettes; and episodes from the Old Testament in the pendentives. Julius II inaugurated the vast work on All Saint's Day 1512 and it excited great admiration.

During Clement VII de' Medici's papacy the idea of painting the altar wall with a monumental scene of the *Last Judgement* was already under discussion. Once again, the great Michelangelo took on the task and created a shocking and visionary masterpiece. The scenes already frescoed on the great wall had to be destroyed to accommodate the new commission. These lost scenes included the *Assumption of the Virgin* by Pietro Perugino, the series of the first *Popes* and Michelangelo's own *Ancestors of Christ* in the lunettes. The maestro worked on the project from 1536 to 1541. Michelangelo worked on the project from 1536 to 1541.

The most recent restoration of all Michelangelo's work in the chapel was carried out at intervals over a period of twenty years from 1979 to 1999, bringing back the wonderful and surprising palette of original colours.

The Sistine Chapel is also widely known because it is the place where the conclave of Cardinals meets to elect the new Pope.

Fifteenth-century frescoes

In 1481 Sixtus IV began to invite renowned painters to work at the heart of Christianity in the Sistine Chapel. Pietro Perugino, Sandro Botticelli, Cosimo Rosselli, Bartolomeo della Gatta and Luca Signorelli along with their pupils worked together on a magnificent decorative project aimed at exalting the Church and Christ's message of salvation.

The decision was made to decorate the middle tier of the walls in the Sistine Chapel with a narrative cycle of episodes of the lives of Moses and Christ to give shape and tangible form to God's faith in humanity, first with the Israelites and then with Christ's Church. There was, of course, solid logic and refined parallels in the choice of the episodes with Moses and Christ representing old and new Law.

The stories originally began on the altar wall with scenes depicting the *Finding of Moses in the Nile* and the *Birth of Christ*, although these were destroyed to make way for Michelangelo's *Last Judgement*. The opposite wall held the *Dispute over the Body of Moses* and the *Resurrection*, also lost when an architrave over the door of the chapel collapsed. These scenes were repainted in the Mannerist era by Matteo da Lecce and Hendrick van den Broeck respectively.

The Sistine painters each kept to their own styles and techniques, although they all agreed to respect a series of precise iconographic rules so as to guarantee the consistency of the scenery, the colour palette and the identifiability of the main figures. Trompe l'oeil drapes were painted on the lower tier and a series of full-length portraits of the twenty-eight Popes after Peter were frescoed in the areas between the windows above.

Trompe l'oeil drapes on the walls

Pietro Perugino, *Moses' Journey into Egypt*

Sandro Botticelli, *Stories of the Life of Moses*

Pietro Perugino, *Baptism of Christ*

Domenico Ghirlandaio, *Vocation of the First Apostles*, whole and detail of the young bystanders

Ceiling

Michelangelo Buonarroti painted the vast ceiling of the Sistine Chapel between 1508 and 1512 with a break around halfway through which gave him the chance to correct his errors of judgement. In spite of the experience he had acquired at the Ghirlandaio workshop in Florence when he was little more than child, the enormity of the task of setting up a worksite of this magnitude must have been overwhelming. Michelangelo tried his best to avoid the task but Pope Julius II was intent on taking a risk on the debuting artist whose extraordinary hands had already created masterpieces such as the *Pietà* sculpted for St. Peter's Basilica nearby, as well as the famous *David*.

Michelangelo's frescoes replaced the existing, simple starry-blue sky painted by Piermatteo d'Amelia. In the stunning new project, framed by a magnificent trompe l'oeil architectural structure, episodes from the Book of Genesis are narrated in the middle section; episodes of salvation are painted in the four corner pendentives; and the *Ancestors of Christ* stand in the lunettes along with the superb seated figures of the *Prophets* and *Sibyls*.

The episodes from the Book of Genesis depict the *Separation of Light and Darkness*, the *Creation of the Sun, the Moon and the Plants*, the *Separation of Land from Water*, the *Creation of Adam*, the *Creation of Eve*, *Original Sin*, *Noah's Sacrifice*, the *Flood*, and the *Drunkenness of Noah*. The corner pendentives illustrate four stories from the Old Testament which show God's interception to protect the chosen people from harm: the *Bronze Serpent*, *David and Goliath*, *Judith and Holofernes* and the *Punishment of Haman*. The spandrels and lunettes underneath hold the *Ancestors of Christ*, painted with extraordinary creativity in various stances according to St. Matthew's Gospel. The vast portrayal is completed by the mighty figures of the *Prophets* and *Sibyls* who, in Hebrew and Pagan tradition, prophesied the coming of Christ the Saviour.

Ceiling of the
Sistine Chapel

Michelangelo, *Separation of Light and Darkness*

Michelangelo, *Creation of the Sun, the Moon and the Plants*

Michelangelo, *Creation of Adam*
on the following pages: Michelangelo, *Original Sin and the Expulsion from Paradise*

Michelangelo, *Flood*

Michelangelo, *Punishment of Haman*

Michelangelo, *Bronze Serpent*

on the following pages: Michelangelo, *Prophet Jonah*

DELPHICA

Michelangelo, *Delphic Sibyl*

LIBICA

Michelangelo, *Libyan Sibyl*

ZACHERIAS

Michelangelo, *Prophet Zechariah*

Michelangelo, *Prophet Isaiah*

Last Judgement

Twenty years after painting the ceiling Michelangelo's ingenious skill returned in all its glory to the Sistine Chapel. Pope Clement VII commissioned the *Last Judgement* to go on the altar wall, although he only lived to see the first preparatory drawings and ideas. In spite of the Pontiff's death the project went ahead and Paul III Farnese confirmed the artist's appointment. Michelangelo began painting on the scaffolding in 1536 and completed the masterpiece in 1541.

As soon as it was uncovered the *Last Judgement* excited great admiration but it also caused a sensation which soon led to profuse and harsh criticism of the artist. No one doubted the ingeniousness and unsurpassed artistic skill of the composition, but the sheer quantity of nude figures, many of which were in suggestive and provocative positions, roused anger from most members of the curia.

Fortunately the fresco wasn't demolished but the curia chose to amend the scene with the famous "breeches" (braghettoni) painted by Daniele da Volterra, incongruous flowing drapes positioned in such a way as to censor the nudity.

The magnificent composition extends outwards around the dominant, full-length figure of Christ the Judge. The Virgin Mary sits nestled almost fearfully by his side while the pure rose-coloured saints in paradise circle around them as far as the eye can see. Angels fly above with the symbols of the Passion, the large cross and the column clearly visible. Lower down on a cloud more angels awaken the dead with their trumpets. Called up one by one, the bodies rise from their graves and come into the presence of the supreme Judge. The extraordinary and unforgettable gesture made by Christ decrees the eternal judgement: the elect, helped by angels and martyrs, rise up into paradise and the damned fall inexorably towards hell where demon torturers lie in wait to seize them. The depiction of hell with the boat of Charon ferrying the damned souls and Minos judging their sins is a clear translation into images of scenes written by Dante Alighieri in the *Divine Comedy*.

Michelangelo, *Last Judgement*, detail of Christ the Judge and the Virgin Mary surrounded by a Host of Saints

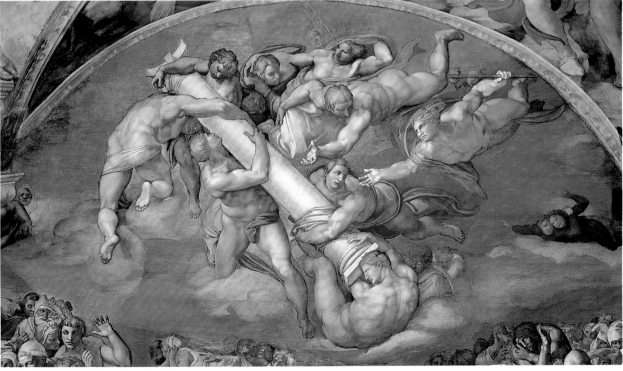

Michelangelo, *Last Judgement*, left and right lunettes: Angels with the Instruments of the Passion

Michelangelo, *Last Judgement*, detail of Trumpet-Playing Angels and Angels with the Book of the Elect and the Book of the Damned

Michelangelo, *Last Judgement*, detail of the Damned

on the following pages: Michelangelo, *Last Judgement*, detail of the Gates of Hell with the Boat of Charon and Minos, the Infernal Judge

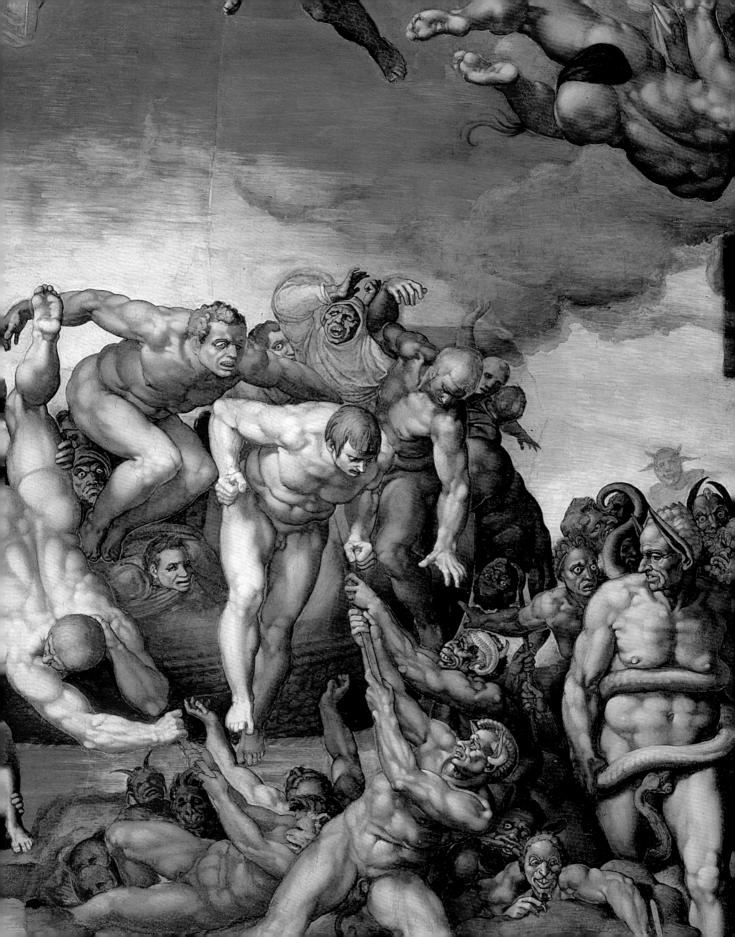

Museums of the Vatican Apostolic Library

The earliest collections of this institution are traditionally attributed to the great humanist sensibilities of Pope Nicholas V (1447–1455), who surrounded himself with men of letters and artists such as Leon Battista Alberti, Marsilio Ficino and Fra Angelico.

The Vatican Library was institutionalised in 1475 under Sixtus IV when Bartolomeo Secchi, known as Platina, was named as its first prefect.

The constant growth of the collections necessitated continual expansion work. A new building was constructed by the architect Domenico Fontana who designed a transversal wing to cut across the Belvedere Courtyard. The wonderful Sistine Salon was at the heart of the new structure; it was conceived as a reading room and richly frescoed with depictions of the most important libraries of antiquity, the councils of the Church and scenes exalting the actions of Nicholas V during his papacy.

In view of the library's constant growth and consequent need for more space, the whole of Bramante's west wing was progressively taken up by the collections leading to the creation of Sixtus V's Rooms, Paul V's Rooms, the Gallery of Urban VIII, Alexander VIII's Room and the Clementine Gallery, all furnished with storage cupboards to hold the works of art which had come into the library's museums over the centuries.

Good Shepherd
c. 300 AD

Pius Christian Museum

The Pius Christian Museum contains collections of Christian antiquities which, until 1963, were on display in the Lateran Palace before being transferred to the Vatican by order of Pope John XXIII.

Pope Pius IX founded the first Christian Lateran Museum in 1854, two years after the creation of the Sacred Archaeology Commission (Commissione di Archeologia Sacra) which had the task of managing the excavations in the catacombs and overseeing their conservation; the finds which could not be kept on site were sent to the museum. The museum's current layout was established by Giuseppe Marchi and Giovanni Battista De Rossi. Some of the most well-known works in the collection include the *Good Shepherd* and the so-called *Dogmatic Sarcophagus*, decorated on the front with the portraits of the couple for whom it was intended, surrounded by scenes from the Old and New Testaments.

Sarcophagus of the Two Brothers
from San Paolo fuori le Mura, first half of the 4th century BC

Dogmatic Sarcophagus
first half of the 4th century AD

Gregorian Profane Museum

The Gregorian Profane Museum was founded in 1844 in the Lateran Palace under Pope Gregory XVI (1831–1846). It was later transferred to the Vatican by order of Pope John XXIII when the layout of the works was modernised, although the collections were only opened to the public in the 1970s.

The museum includes artefacts from most of the excavations and discovery sites in the Papal States and contains masterpieces of Greek art as well as Roman copies and originals from the Imperial era. The museum is divided into five main sections: fragments of sculptures and original Greek reliefs; first to third-century AD Roman copies and reworkings of Greek originals; Roman sculptures (mainly busts and altars) from the first century and early second century; sarcophagi with mythological scenes, masks and festoons and scenes of daily life; and Roman sculptures from the second and third century.

The most important works include the *Funerary Stele with a Young Athlete*, the *Altar of the Vicomagistri* and the *Chiaramonti Niobid,* which is thought to be based on the group by Scopas or Praxiteles. The museum also holds a large mosaic with athletes from the Baths of Caracalla.

Chiaramonti Niobid reworking after a late-Classical era Greek original, late 2nd century BC

151

Missionary Ethnological Museum

The Missionary Ethnological Museum was founded by Pope Pius XI in 1926 after the Universal Missionary Exhibition in the Holy Year of 1925. The collections were put on display in the Lateran Palace and then inaugurated by Pope Paul VI in 1973.

Tomkio ceremonial pirogue
Melanesia, Salomon Islands, Choiseul
19th–20th century

The collections contain almost one hundred thousand objects from all five continents. Some noteworthy pieces include the suit of samurai armour (Japan), the statue of the god *Rongo* (Oceania), the Japanese paintings, the African fabric and the *Plumed Snake* or *Quetzalcoatl*, a pre-Columbian divinity from the Americas.

Suit of samurai armour, Japan late Edo period (1615–1868)– second half of the 19th century

*Wooden statue of
the god Rongo*
Polynesia,
Mangarewa Islands,
late 18th century

Carriage Museum

This museum began to take shape in 1968 and Pope Paul VI inaugurated the collections in 1973. It contains the beautiful sedan chairs, carriages, berlins and cars used by the Popes and other dignitaries of the Papal Court in a vast underground room. Particularly interesting items include the *Berlin Grand Touring Carriage* built for Pope Leo XII and the cars: the Citroën *Lictoria Sex* and the Mercedes Benz.

Another exhibit worth seeing is the model of the first steam locomotive of the Italian State Railway to come across the border into the Vatican State. Construction began on the new Vatican Railway in 1929 and it opened officially in 1934.

Citroën Lictoria Sex
gift from André Citroën to Pius XI in 1930

Model of the first locomotive of the Italian State Railway to come into the Vatican City
1932

LEO · XII · PONTIFEX · MAXIMVS · FRONTEM · HANC · RENOVAVIT · PONT · AN · I ·

PIVS · IIII · MEDICES · MEDIOLANEN · PONTIFEX · MAXIMVS ·
INNEMORE · PALATII · VATICANI · PORTICVM ·
APSIDATAM · CVM · COLVMNIS · NVMIDICIS · FONTIBVS ·
LYMPHÆO · IMMINENTEM · E · REGIONE · AREAE ·
EXTRVXIT · ANN · SAL · MDLXI ·

THE VATICAN GARDENS

Vatican Gardens

The Vatican Gardens cover most of the Vatican City and extend up to the top of the Vatican Hill behind St. Peter's Basilica, Palazzo del Governato and the Vatican Museums. They are adorned with groves, avenues, sculptures, artificial grottoes and fountains.

The gardens are a place for the Pope to rest and relax, closed off and protected by the ancient fortified walls built by Leo IV (847–855). The walls have been frequently modernised over the centuries although the most significant improvements were carried out between the sixteenth and seventeenth centuries when the park was enriched with geometrically laid out gardens, buildings and monumental fountains.

on page 156:
Casina of Pius IV

Fountain of the Eagle

Access to the gardens is subject to special passes issued by the Vatican Gendarmerie. There are important institutions of the state in the park such as the Governorate, the State Tribunal, the building of the first broadcasting station of the Vatican Radio designed by Guglielmo Marconi (1931), the Railway Station and a heliport. The gardens are also widely-known for their diverse array of botanical species.

Noteworthy, superbly-decorated buildings include the Palazzina of Pius IX, now the seat of Pontifical Academy of Sciences, the little house or *Casina* of Pius IV, built in 1588 by Pirri Ligorio with an elaborate stuccoed façade, the *Fountain of the Eagle*, built by Jan van Santen (Giovanni Vasanzio, 1550–1621), and the *Fountain of the Sacrament*.

View of the Gardens

THE VATICAN